March 9, 2015

# BAKING—EASY, ELEGANT & EGGLESS

Dearest Carolyn,
you are such a
sweet being — enjoy
these sweets.
Love to you & happy
baking,
Prayzna

# BAKING

## *Easy, Elegant & Eggless*

ARLENE KEZWER

## Sterling Paperbacks

An imprint of
Sterling Publishers (P) Ltd.
Regd. Office: A-59, Okhla Industrial Area, Phase-II,
New Delhi-110020. Cin: U22110PB1964PTC002569
Tel: 26387070, 26386209; Fax: 91-11-26383788
E-mail: mail@sterlingpublishers.com
www.sterlingpublishers.com

**BAKING:** *Easy, Elegant & Eggless*
ISBN 978-81-207-9652-2
Copyright © 2015 Arlene Kezwer
First edition 2015

Design and layout by Jonty Hayes
Photography by Arlene Kezwer, Barbara Mulroney, Ellen Reitman
Original artwork copyright © Stephen Aitken
Editor Susan Cowan

Printed in India
*Printed and Published by* Sterling Publishers Pvt. Ltd.,
New Delhi-110 020

With the utmost respect and appreciation I dedicate this book to Swami Shyam. He has given me the greatest gift in life, the vision of Oneness, the knowledge that the source of all creation is one eternal life force. I am supremely fortunate to have Swamiji's presence in my life. He has been my inspiration and ideal in everything—including this book.

# Contents

# Teatime Recipes

# Cookies & Squares

## Pies & Pastries

## Icings & Glazes

# *Acknowledgements*

Thanks go first to my husband, Glen Kezwer, for his constant support, assistance and unfailing good nature, not only in this project but in every aspect of life.

I would like to give special thanks to Stephen Aitken, Susan Cowan, Barbara Mulroney and Ellen Reitman. Thanks also to Judith Forward, Surinder Ghai, Jonty Hayes, Kristen Jarden, Andrea Jutras, Mary McGugan, Yuli Mazliah, Eric Myhr, Sita Raina, Sarah Randolph, Jill Ronsley, Mayur Sharma, Sherrie Wade and the many friends and family members who have showered their encouragement and enthusiasm to see this book reach its finale. Every aspect of this book received generous expert attention—from photography, editing, layout and design, proofreading and general guidance—without which I would not have succeeded in this endeavour.

# Introduction

It is a pleasure to present these recipes to you. I've been baking and offering these treats to friends and family for many years, and they are always well received and fully enjoyed. Some are rich and sumptuous. Others have been created with a view to health and a diet low in fat. Still other recipes are traditional favourites, like brownies, chocolate-chip cookies and scones. A few may be included in a breakfast, lunch or dinner, rather than as desserts.

The one thing they have in common is that they are all made without eggs.

If you think that baking a cake without eggs means it won't rise high or be light in texture, you will be surprised and delighted by these recipes. If you think cookies, biscuits and squares need eggs to be successful, try these recipes and see the results.

Perhaps you don't use eggs for health reasons, such as high cholesterol or food allergies. Maybe you are a vegetarian (these recipes are lacto-vegetarian, making use of dairy products, while some are vegan), or perhaps you just ran out of eggs and don't want to make a trip to the store. Whatever the reason, this unique book offers a wide variety of baked goods—all wonderful and all made without eggs.

The recipes in this book deliver the promise of taste, texture, and total dessert satisfaction, while keeping an eye on the ingredients with a view towards healthy eating. Granted, a few of them contain quite a lot of butter and most use sugar—this is not a health-food cookbook—but most of the recipes use whole wheat flour and many of them call for small amounts of oil. I've experimented with many of the recipes and have decreased the amounts of fat and sugar wherever possible, while still producing successful desserts.

So please turn the pages, see your choices, then go to the kitchen and have fun creating some of these delicious sweets.

# An Explanation of Measures, Ingredients & Temperature

This book is for people all over the world who want to bake without eggs. I come from North America but have spent more time in India than anywhere else. As I began to write up these recipes, there were many fundamental decisions to make: Should the measurements be metric or should I use the measures I had grown up with? Should I use the American and Canadian names for the ingredients, or the Indian? I decided to write the recipes the way I actually measure them, according to the U.S. system, but there is a list of equivalents on page 11. Wherever the Indian names of the ingredients differ from the North American or European, both are given in the glossary. As well as being a practical solution, I hope this adds a touch of interest for you, the reader.

A cup means an 8 oz. or 250 ml measuring cup. Teaspoons and tablespoons are standard measuring items, available in most kitchen shops. Half a cup of butter is close enough to one stick (U.S.), one pack (India) or 100 grams. Any slight differences will not affect the results of your baking.

**Oven temperatures are frequently inexact. In these recipes I've chosen to express baking temperatures in terms of slow, medium, medium-hot, and hot. A conversion table showing the recommended temperatures with their Celsius and Fahrenheit equivalents can be found on page 11.**

# *About Substituting & Experimenting*

I have been asked if some of these recipes could be made with gluten-free flour, which means without wheat flour. Corn, rice, buckwheat, and chickpea flours are just some of the possibilities you may try in an effort to bake without gluten. Some health-food stores sell gluten-free flour, which is generally a mix of different grains ground into flour. Please note that by making such a major substitution, the results will differ from the original recipe.

Another question frequently asked is whether it's possible to make desserts without sugar. If the ratio of dry ingredients to wet is fairly closely maintained, you can certainly change some of the ingredients and still have good results. Be creative and experiment. If sugar is a health issue for you, then honey will also not be an option. There are a few products, such as stevia, Nutra-sweet and Sugar Free Natura that you can try. Check your health-food store for alternatives. Please note that the taste and texture of your baking may be significantly altered by this substitution.

The other ingredient that people may wish to substitute is butter. If you substitute oil for butter, many of the recipes become vegan, thereby allowing strict vegetarians a chance to try them, as well as addressing the issue of cholesterol. There is a definite difference in the taste and texture of a cake, and especially a cookie, if you switch from butter to oil, but in many cases the result is satisfactory or even excellent. Cakes are more "forgiving" than cookies, allowing for this substitution.

# *Getting Started*

I suggest you read this section carefully before starting to bake. The hints given here will save you time and energy, and will help ensure that your efforts are successful.

When you've chosen the recipe that you wish to bake, read it through carefully before starting. This will save you from realizing half-way through that you don't have one or more of the ingredients in the house. (This suggestion comes from direct experience!) A helpful technique is to assemble all the necessary ingredients on the counter before you begin. Have your measuring cups and spoons ready, your mixing bowls and mixing spoon, and a rubber spatula all at hand, along with the baking pan you'll be using. Measure your dry ingredients and sift them together. Greasing and flouring your baking pan in advance is efficient and saves last minute hassle. Preheat your oven about 10 minutes before starting to bake.

If you've decided to bake at the last minute and don't have a lot of time, choose a recipe that calls for melted butter or oil. Recipes that ask you to cream the butter with the sugar require a little more planning, as the butter needs to be soft but not melted. This can take quite a bit of time with the butter out of the fridge. One helpful hint when trying to soften butter in the winter is to place it near a warm appliance or under an electric light. (But check it often, as it will melt under a direct light.)

When baking more than one item during the same session, there are certain steps of each recipe that you can do at the same time. For example, sift and measure your dry ingredients for each recipe into separate bowls—then you'll be able to clear away the various jars involved in that part of the process. You can also prepare your baking pans at the same time.

If you are planning to bake for a breakfast or a brunch, you can sift all your dry ingredients the night before and leave the bowls covered on the counter. Measure the other ingredients as well, and place them on the counter nearby. You'll be pleasantly surprised at how quickly things will go in the morning. Baking powder, baking soda and powdered egg substitutes are ingredients that cannot be measured out in advance. Any exposure to moisture (even in the air) will cause the powder and soda to begin working; thus they won't have enough rising power left if the recipe is to be baked later.

# About the Ingredients & Your Pantry

Use the freshest ingredients you can find. Quality and freshness make a considerable difference to the finished product. And of course, if the rising agents (baking powder and baking soda) are not fresh, your results will be disappointing.

## Egg Substitutes

Here, I would like to comment on the subject of egg substitutes—the item that makes this book unique.

It's helpful to know what purpose eggs serve in any given recipe. In some cases eggs are meant to provide leavening (rising), in some they help to bind the ingredients together. They can also be used to add moistness and density where wanted. You can choose how to replace the eggs depending on what they are needed for. Applesauce or mashed bananas may be used when moistness is needed, but they will create a denser result, and bananas add a definite flavour. Yogurt or curd works well in recipes that require moisture, but they will add a tangy quality, especially if the yogurt is a bit strong. As you look through the recipes, you'll see that many do not require any egg substitute at all.

Almost any store-bought egg replacer can be used for all purposes. Try to find one that does not call for more than 2 tablespoons of water for each egg that is replaced. If such a product is unavailable to you, there are various homemade recipes for egg substitutes. The one I recommend is:

**For each egg place 1½ teaspoons of corn starch (corn flour in India) or custard powder in a cup. Add a pinch of baking powder and a smaller pinch of baking soda. Then add two tablespoons of water to the dry ingredients and mix quickly and thoroughly. Mix only when you are about to use—not in advance.**

## Flour

Most of the recipes in this book use whole wheat pastry flour. In India, superfine *atta* is a close equivalent that will work well. Wherever the recipe calls for white flour, *maida* is the equivalent. If you can't find superfine *atta*, you can mix half *maida* with half *roti atta*. In other places you can mix half white flour and half whole wheat flour, if you can't find whole wheat pastry flour. The occasional recipe calls for corn flour. This means *makhi atta*, or corn meal, not corn starch.

# An Important Point about Flour

Flour is a lively ingredient and every time you buy it, it may be a bit different from the last batch. Even the time of year (especially the monsoon) may alter the amount of liquid that flour absorbs. This means that the amount of liquid required to create a batter of the desired texture and thickness may differ a bit each time. Therefore, the amount of liquid listed in the recipes is approximate. This is an important point, but don't be daunted by the idea that you won't know how much to use. Start with a bit less than the recipe calls for, adding it slowly and stirring your batter between additions of liquid. In some cases, the amount in the recipe will be too little and you may need to add up to ¼ or even ½ cup extra. In the recipe descriptions, I've tried to give an idea of what the dough or batter should be like, so you'll know how much liquid to use. And be assured—the more you bake, the more you'll come to trust your own judgement. That's part of the fun of baking, and soon you'll be making variations to the recipes based on your own tastes, or even the ingredients you have in the house. Baking is a creative process and a lot of fun too, so put on some nice music and enjoy yourself!

When measuring flour, spoon it lightly into the measuring cup—don't pack it down. Always sift your flour before measuring as it makes a difference to the texture of the dessert, as well as ensuring cleanliness.

# Sugar and Other Sweeteners

Wherever sugar is indicated, use either **granulated sugar**, **caster sugar** or **ground sugar**—the large-grained Indian sugar will not give the desired result. This large-grained sugar may be ground in a coffee or spice grinder if you can't find ground or caster sugar in a store.

Where recipes call for **brown sugar**, try to find a brand that is not too granular, but rather one that is soft and packs easily in the measuring cup. If an imported brand such as Tate & Lyle's is available, it's worth the expense. In Canada and the U.S. soft brown sugar is found in every grocery store. You may want to use light brown sugar in some recipes and dark brown in others.

**Icing sugar**, or **confectioner's sugar** as it is sometimes called, will be needed for making icing as well as for a few baked items.

A few of the recipes call for **golden syrup** or **honey**. Both are good to have on hand in your pantry. **Molasses** is called for in a few recipes, though it is less available in India than in the West. If you can't find molasses, you can easily make your own. In a heavy saucepan, place approximately 500 grams of *gur* and ¼ cup of water. Heat over a low flame, stirring often. In just a few minutes you will have a golden-brown syrup. Pour this through a tea strainer into a clean glass jar, as *gur* has occasional bits of grit in it. When it has cooled, skim off any foam. *Gur* syrup can be kept in the jar for quite some time. **Shakhar** may also be used to make molasses. Please note that both honey and molasses bake a bit more quickly than sugar, so be careful that these recipes don't burn.

# *Other Ingredients*

The following are other ingredients that are frequently used in these recipes and helpful to have on hand in your panty:

**Raisins**, either light or dark are fine. If you are buying raisins that are sold loose, they will need to be cleaned and washed. First, sort through them picking out any debris. Then wash by placing the raisins in a large bowl and pour warm, filtered water over them. Swish them about with your hands and then lift the raisins out of the bowl into another bowl or a colander. You'll see the dirt at the bottom of the first bowl when you pour the water off. Repeat this process until the water is clear and the bowl is clean. Let them drain for a few minutes and then spread on a tea towel or clean cloth to air dry. When fully dry, store in a jar.

**Walnuts** should be stored in the fridge. Be sure to check that there are no stray pieces of shell going into the recipe. **Coconut powder**, **chopped dates**, **chocolate chips** and **candied ginger** are all standard baking items. **Vanilla extract** is a must, and **almond extract** is a useful item. If you can get real vanilla beans you can make your own **vanilla sugar**. Just slit the bean down the centre and place it in a jar of sugar. In two weeks you will have an amazing, subtle treat. You may use vanilla sugar in any recipe, but it is especially useful in recipes like shortbreads, where no liquid is called for, yet you want the taste of vanilla. **Cinnamon**, **nutmeg**, **cloves** and **ginger**, all ground to a fine powder will be used often. **Unsweetened cocoa powder** is another item to stock in your baking pantry. Any brand of **baking powder** is fine, and **baking soda** is known in India as either *meetha* soda or sodium bicarbonate.

In North America, grocery stores and supermarkets stock salted and unsalted **butter**. I prefer unsalted, but in India butter is generally salted. Because of this I've not included salt in any of the recipes. Salt is not really necessary in baked goods, and these days many people are eating less salt. Where **oil** is called for, a light, neutral tasting one is recommended, such as safflower, sunflower, or rice bran oil. Oils such as canola, olive, sesame, and mustard have too strong a flavour for desserts.

# *Recommended Baking Equipment*

You will probably find that most of the equipment used in these recipes is already in your kitchen. If you do need something, baking equipment is readily available in kitchen stores everywhere, as well as on-line.

A set of measuring cups and spoons is essential. One or two large stainless steel or plastic mixing bowls and a couple of smaller ones will be used in most recipes. A wire whisk and wooden spoons are helpful. A sifter is needed, but a simple sieve is just fine. A rubber spatula is a useful baking tool, used for scraping all your batter from the bowl easily. A metal or hard rubber spatula for lifting cookies from the baking tray to the cooling rack is another small item you will need. A pastry brush is also helpful.

Good quality baking pans go a long way towards making your efforts successful. Many of the cakes in this book are baked in a 10-inch round tube pan, sometimes referred to as a bundt pan. Some are made in 9- or 10-inch round layer-cake pans. The squares and brownies are made in an 8- or 9-inch square pan; a few of the recipes for squares are made in an 8½ x 11-inch pan with ½-inch sides. At least one cookie sheet is needed if you wish to make any of the cookie recipes. A standard sized bread pan, muffin tins and a 9-inch pie pan will be required in some of the recipes.

An interesting thing about baking pans is that the type of material they are made of (aluminium, glass, stick-free) affects the baking time and the texture of your finished product. I used to have a very expensive stick-free cake pan. The cakes came out of the pan easily, but they all had a tough, rubbery outer crust. I have other stick-free pans that have never created this problem, so just be aware that certain cake pans may not suit you. If you use glass, slightly reduce the temperature of your oven, as glass tends to bake faster than metal. Aluminium has gotten a bad reputation in recent years, but I don't think you need to be concerned about it in baking pans. Many of my cakes are baked in inexpensive aluminium cake pans because they consistently give good results. Even an aluminium *parath* or a white enamel plate may be used in some recipes, such as fruit crisps or pies.

If you live in an area where a variety of pan sizes and shapes is not available, but you have a good metalwork shop nearby, you can get any size of pan made in sheet metal or aluminium. I've done this many times, and these are among my favourite baking pans. This works especially well for cookie sheets, and you can have them made to fit the exact size of your oven. And lastly, if you can find (or make) a couple of cooling racks you'll find them very helpful.

The only electric items that I use regularly in making these recipes are a hand mixer and a food processor. You can do without them if you don't mind a little extra chopping and hand mixing, but I do recommend you invest in the hand mixer if you start to bake more often. When using a food processor to make dough or mix cake batters, be careful not to over process the ingredients. And there are a couple of recipes in which I just dive in and use my hands for the whole process.

Of course, the most important tool is your oven. The type of oven doesn't matter. I've baked all of these recipes in an electric OTG (oven-toaster-griller) as well as in a tin box oven placed on a gas burner. No doubt this type of oven is old-fashioned, but it works beautifully. The main thing is that your oven should heat evenly and the heat should be adjustable. An important point is to observe whether the shelves in your oven are straight or are at a slant. If they are not straight you will need to turn your pan a few times during the baking. (Or even better, try to get them fixed!) Of course, it is better not to open the oven door too often, but if you are quick and use a light touch, this should not affect your results.

Note: These recipes are not intended for microwave ovens.

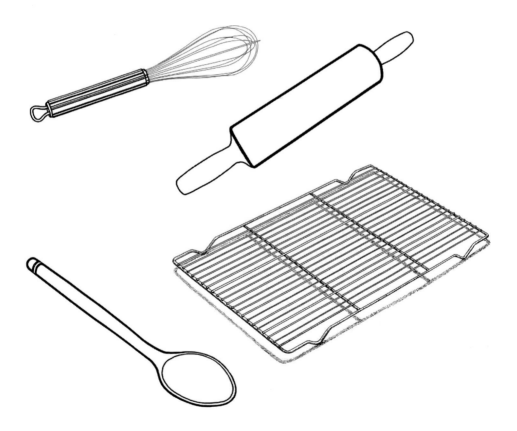

# Temperature Conversion Chart

| Description | Celsius | Fahrenheit |
|-------------|---------|------------|
| Slow | 150–160 | 300–325 |
| Medium | 180–190 | 350–375 |
| Medium-Hot | 190–200 | 375–400 |
| Hot | 200–230 | 400–450 |

# Volume Conversion Chart

| US & Canadian Measures | Metric |
|------------------------|--------|
| ⅛ teaspoon | 0.5 ml |
| ¼ teaspoon | 1.23 ml |
| ½ teaspoon | 2.5 ml |
| 1 teaspoon | 5 ml |
| 1 tablespoon | 15 ml |
| 2 tablespoons (1 ounce) | 30 ml |
| ¼ cup (2 ounces) | 60 ml |
| ⅓ cup (2.67 ounces) | 75 ml |
| ½ cup (4 ounces) | 120 ml |
| ¾ cup (6 ounces) | 180 ml |
| 1 cup (8 ounces) | 240 ml |

# Cakes

# About Cakes

There's nothing quite so elegant as a gorgeous iced and decorated cake carried out at the end of a meal. When the word "baking" or "dessert" is mentioned, many people automatically think of cake. These days, cakes are sometimes treated as an art form, with television shows following their production and delivery. There are so many kinds of cakes, so many flavours, so many possibilities to play with; here is a comprehensive and varied selection of recipes for your enjoyment. A few are iced, some glazed, a couple have a classic "streusel" topping and others are just dusted lightly with icing sugar. In each case, you can decide how you want to top off the recipe.

There's a lot of scope for creativity in cake making, but do stick to the proportions of dry to liquid ingredients. As far as the flavours go, when you become comfortable with a recipe, you will be able to alter it to suit your own taste. Certain cakes are really better eaten the day they are baked, while many are fine and may even have a better texture on the second day. And even when you think your leftover cake is stale, it may be perfect for making a quick trifle—just crumble the cake into a bowl, pour some custard over it, dot it with jam and slices of fruit, and you'll have a wonderful dessert!

I would like to give a few hints about removing your cakes from their pans. Preparing your baking pans before filling them with the batter is an important step. You'll want to LIGHTLY oil or butter the pan and then dust it with flour. Spoon about 1 tablespoon of flour into the greased pan and shake it all over—up, down and around, trying not to leave any bare spots. Then, with the heel of your palm, firmly knock out any excess flour. If you use too much butter or oil in preparing the pan, your cake is more likely to burn (almost fry) and will be much more difficult to remove from the pan.

When your cake is baked, place it on the cooling rack. Let it rest for about 10 minutes, then gently but firmly shake the pan to see if the cake comes away easily from the sides. If it does not, take a sharp knife and very gently go around the cake's outside edge (and the inside too, if you've used a tube pan), pressing the cake very slightly away from the pan to make sure it has not stuck anywhere. Holding the cake pan with a pot holder, firmly rap the edge of the pan on the heel of your palm, going around the whole pan until the cake becomes loosened. Now the cake is ready to turn out of the pan. Take the cooling rack or a plate, hold it against the cake pan and turn the pan upside down. Your cake should slide out easily and will be upside down. Hold another cooling rack against the cake and flip it over so that the cake is right side up. There are many excellent websites you can consult to see this done. Cool completely before icing.

# Fresh Apple Cake

This surprising recipe yields one of my favourite cakes—the raw apples practically melt into the batter. It is easy to make and always successful. Serve with or without an icing, a glaze or a streusel topping. It's also delicious served with ice cream or vanilla custard. Bake in a preheated medium oven in a greased and floured 10-inch tube pan. **Serves 8 to 10.**

*1 cup brown sugar*

*½ cup oil*

*substitute for 2 eggs*

*¼ cup water*

*1 tsp vanilla extract*

*2 full cups finely minced apple*

*2¼ cups whole wheat pastry flour*

*1 tsp baking soda*

*1 tsp baking powder*

*1 tsp cinnamon*

*½ tsp nutmeg*

*⅛ tsp cloves*

In a large mixing bowl, beat together the sugar, oil, egg substitute, water and vanilla. Stir in the apples.

In a separate bowl, sift together the flour, baking soda and baking powder. Mix in the spices. Fold the dry ingredients into the wet. If the batter seems too stiff (it should be fairly thick, but not dry) add a bit more water until it seems right.

Spoon into your prepared cake pan and bake for about 30 minutes or until a toothpick inserted near the centre comes out clean. Cool on a wire rack and remove from the pan after about 10 minutes. If you plan to ice or glaze the cake, let it cool completely. Pictured here with a simple vanilla glaze drizzled over it.

# Chocolate Pudding Cake

This cake is like a little bit of kitchen chemistry. It's delicious and quite surprising. Be sure to let it cool enough before removing it from the pan, or the pudding on the bottom will be too runny and hot. Bake in a preheated medium oven in a greased and floured 10-inch round cake pan. **Serves 6 to 8.**

⅓ cup butter

½ cup milk

1 cup whole wheat pastry flour

1½ tsp baking powder

2 T cocoa powder

¾ cup sugar

1 tsp vanilla extract

¾ cup brown sugar

1¾ cups boiling water

In a saucepan, stir the butter and milk together over a low flame and let the butter melt. While this mixture cools, sift the flour, baking powder and 1 tablespoon of cocoa powder together into a mixing bowl. Stir the dry ingredients into the butter and milk, along with the sugar and vanilla. (If you use a large enough pot for the milk and butter you won't need to use and clean a separate mixing bowl.) Stir just enough to make sure all the ingredients are mixed together. Spread this batter into your prepared cake pan.

Cover the top of the batter with the brown sugar and sprinkle with the remaining 1 T of cocoa. Slowly pour the boiling water over it. Place carefully in the oven and bake for approximately 40 minutes. When the cake has cooled for about 30 minutes, remove from the pan and turn it over to continue cooling on a rack. You'll have a delicious cake with chocolate pudding on top!

# Chocolate Cake

This is a favourite party cake, chocolatey and rich. It can be made in a tube pan, in layer cake pans or as cupcakes. Frosted and decorated, spread with thickened strawberry jam and whipped cream, a fruit coulis or just sprinkled with icing sugar—whatever you decide, it won't fail to please. Bake in a preheated medium oven in a greased and floured 9-inch round cake pan or a 9-inch tube pan. **Serves 8.**

*½ cup cocoa powder*

*1 cup boiling water*

*1⅓ cups whole wheat pastry flour*

*2 tsp baking powder*

*½ cup soft butter*

*1 cup sugar*

*substitute for 2 eggs*

*2 tsp vanilla*

In a small metal bowl, pour the boiling water over the cocoa powder and mix well. Let this mixture cool.

In another bowl, sift the flour and baking powder together and set aside.

In a third bowl, beat the butter and sugar until creamy. Add the egg substitute and vanilla, and beat again. Mix in the water and cocoa mixture and beat. Finally, fold in the flour and baking powder.

Pour the batter into your prepared cake pan. Bake for about 20 minutes, or until the cake begins to pull away from the sides of the pan. To test if it is done, a cake tester or toothpick inserted in the centre should come out clean. Cool the cake in its pan on a rack for about 10 minutes, then remove from the pan and continue to cool before applying any icing or topping.

The recipe can be doubled to make an impressive layer cake.

# Coconut Mango Cake

This is a moist cake that may be kept simple or dressed-up quite a lot. Either way, it's delicious and will delight your guests. It is shown here adorned with mango slices. Kiwi fruit also works well and looks beautiful, as do strawberry halves. Bake in a preheated medium oven in a greased and floured 9- or 10-inch round cake pan. **Serves 10 to 12.**

¾ cup butter

1 cup sugar

1½ cups sour cream,
 yogurt or curd

1 tsp vanilla extract

2 cups whole wheat
 pastry flour

1 tsp baking soda

1 tsp baking powder

1 cup flaked or
 desiccated coconut

ripe mango slices
 for decoration

Cream the butter and sugar together in a large bowl. Mix in the yogurt and vanilla and beat until light and fluffy. In a separate bowl, sift the flour with the baking soda and baking powder. Stir in the coconut. Add the dry mixture to the wet in a few batches, mixing lightly between additions.

Pour the batter into your prepared cake pan and bake for approximately 30–35 minutes, or until a toothpick or cake tester comes out clean. Cool for 10 minutes on a rack, and then turn out of the pan and continue cooling. Use your choice of icing when the cake is completely cooled.

Optional: Bake in layer cake pans and fill the centre with a dripped curd or cream cheese filling that has been lightly sweetened. Another option is to make cupcakes that are individually iced and topped with candied or fresh fruit.

# Coconut & Date Loaf

This recipe is simply delicious, especially for those who like coconut. It's moist, rich and easy to make. It has a very tender texture, so let it cool completely in the pan before cutting and transferring to a serving plate. Bake in a preheated medium oven in a greased and floured loaf pan. **Serves 8.**

*½ cup boiling water*

*1 cup dates cut small*

*½ cup butter*

*½ cup sugar*

*substitute for 1 egg*

*1 cup whole wheat pastry flour*

*1 tsp baking powder*

*¼ cup coconut*

In a small bowl, pour the boiling water over the dates and let stand for 15 minutes. In another bowl cream the butter and sugar, then add the egg substitute and beat.

In a third bowl, sift the flour and the baking powder. Into the bowl of butter and sugar, stir the flour, baking powder, coconut and lastly the dates, including the water they have been soaking in.

Spoon the batter into your prepared baking pan and bake for about 30 minutes or until golden brown. The loaf should start to pull away from the sides of the pan. Cool on a rack and slice the loaf in the pan when totally cool.

You can serve this plain, with a sifting of icing sugar, a vanilla glaze or any icing of your choice.

This recipe may also be made as squares, baked in a 9-inch square pan.

# Banana Chocolate-Chip Cake

This is a really delicious cake, moist and sweet without being overly rich. Use ripe bananas to ensure your cake has that sweet banana flavour. Bake in a preheated medium oven in a greased and floured 9- or 10-inch round cake pan or a tube pan. **Serves 8 to 10.**

¾ cup mashed bananas

¼ cup oil

¼ cup butter

1¼ cups curd or yogurt

1½ tsp vanilla

1 cup sugar

2 cups whole wheat
  pastry flour

a pinch of nutmeg

2 tsp baking powder

1 scant tsp baking soda

1 cup dark chocolate
  chips

In a large bowl, mix the mashed bananas with the oil, yogurt, butter and vanilla. Stir in the sugar and set this mixture aside.

In another bowl, sift the flour with the baking powder and baking soda and stir in the nutmeg. Add the chocolate chips and stir again. Make a well in the centre of the dry ingredients and pour all of the liquid ingredients into it. Stir gently until the dry and wet ingredients are integrated, but do not overmix.

Pour this mixture into your prepared cake pan and bake for 30–35 minutes, or until a toothpick or cake tester comes out clean. Cool on a rack for about 10 minutes before turning out. When the cake has cooled, you may decorate it with the icing or glaze of your choice.

# Cinnamon Tea Cake

This small cake is light and moist, perfect served with a cup of tea or coffee and very simple to make. Like all tea cakes, it's best eaten the same day it is baked. Bake in a preheated medium oven in a greased and floured 9-inch round cake pan. **Serves 6.**

⅓ cup butter

⅔ cup sugar

1 tsp vanilla extract

substitute for 1 egg

1¼ cups whole wheat
  pastry flour

2 tsp baking powder

⅓-½ cup milk


1 T melted butter

1 T castor sugar

1 tsp cinnamon

In a large bowl, beat together the butter, sugar, vanilla and egg substitute. In a separate bowl, sift the flour and baking powder together.

Stir the dry ingredients into the butter mixture, alternating with additions of milk. When you have a smooth batter, spread it into your prepared cake pan. Bake for about 30 minutes or until the sides start to pull away from the pan and the cake has a golden colour.

Cool in the pan for about 10 minutes, then turn the cake out onto the cooling rack. At this stage, using a pastry brush, brush the top of the cake with the remaining melted butter and sprinkle immediately with the sugar and cinnamon. Allow the cake to cool completely before cutting and serving.

This recipe may be doubled and used to make a very nice layer cake.

# Classic White Cake

This is a very simple, versatile recipe. Delicious as is, it can be varied with additions such as spices, raisins, nuts, chocolate chips, orange or lemon zest, almond extract or anything that strikes your fancy. Bake in a preheated medium oven in a greased and floured 9- or 10-inch round cake pan. **Serves 8 to 10.**

¼ cup oil

¼ cup butter

1 cup sugar

2 cups whole wheat pastry flour

1 scant tsp baking soda

2 tsp baking powder

substitute for 2 eggs

approximately 1 cup milk or yogurt or curd

2 tsp vanilla

In a large bowl, cream the oil, butter and sugar together well with a wooden spoon or beat with a hand mixer.

In a separate bowl, sift the dry ingredients together and set aside.

Add the milk, egg substitute and vanilla into the oil, butter and sugar mixture and beat well. Add the dry ingredients to the wet mixture in two or three batches, mixing after each addition. At this point, the batter should not be beaten, but gently mixed. It should be medium thick—not dry but not too runny. Alternatively, this may all be done in a food processor, but be sure not to overprocess the ingredients.

Spoon the batter into your prepared cake pan and bake for approximately 30 minutes or until the cake begins to pull away from the sides of the pan and a toothpick or cake tester comes out of the centre clean. Set the cake on a wire rack to cool for about 10 minutes before turning it out of the pan.

Allow the cake to cool completely before icing it or topping with a glaze. For a change, cut the cake and spoon fruit syrup or stewed fruit over each serving. Pictured with Honey-Chocolate Sauce (recipe on page 101).

# Apple & Nut Pie

This is a simple dessert that is very low in fat. It's perfect when you want something sweet for just a few people. Technically, this is not a pie; rather, it is a small cake made in a lightly greased 9-inch pie tin. Bake in a preheated medium oven. **Serves 6.**

*½ cup whole wheat
  pastry flour*

*1 tsp baking powder*

*½ cup sugar*

*1 T melted butter*

*substitute for 1 egg
  + 1 T water*

*1 tsp vanilla*

*1 cup peeled, finely
  chopped apples*

*1 cup finely chopped
  pecans or walnuts*

*½ tsp cinnamon*

In a small bowl, sift the flour and baking powder and set aside. In a large bowl, beat the sugar, butter, egg substitute and vanilla. Stir the dry ingredients into the butter mixture and fold in the apples, nuts and cinnamon.

Spoon into the prepared pie pan. This is a thick batter that needs to be spread evenly in the pan. Bake for approximately 30 minutes. Cool on a rack and slice in the pan, like a pie. Or turn out onto a cooling rack and when fully cool, spread with apricot jam, as shown in the photo, or sprinkle with sifted icing sugar.

Optional: Replace the butter with oil for a vegan version of this dessert.

# Pumpkin Orange Chocolate Cake

Pumpkin is the healthy, surprise ingredient in this moist, delicious cake. Only the most discerning palate would ever guess it's there. Bake in a preheated medium oven in a greased and floured 9-inch round cake pan. **Serves 6 to 8.**

*⅓ cup oil or butter*

*2 tsp grated orange zest*

*½ cup + 2 T sugar substitute for 1 egg*

*2 T honey or golden syrup*

*1 cup cooked, mashed pumpkin*

*1½ cups whole wheat pastry flour*

*1 tsp baking powder*

*½ tsp baking soda*

*3 T cocoa powder*

*1 T custard powder*

*⅓ cup orange juice*

In a large bowl, cream the butter or oil (your choice) with the orange zest and sugar. Beat in the egg substitute and honey, then stir in the pumpkin.

Sift the dry ingredients together in a separate bowl. Gradually stir the dry ingredients into the wet ingredients, stirring in the orange juice at intervals.

Pour the batter into the prepared cake pan and bake for approximately 30 minutes, or until a toothpick inserted in the centre comes out clean. Set the cake on a cooling rack for about 10 minutes before turning it out of the pan. Cool completely, then ice or glaze with the topping of your choice, and enjoy.

# Gingerbread Cake

Often described as "comfort food," this delicious, moist cake is a spicy classic that is perfect for any occasion. Bake in a preheated medium oven in a greased and floured 9-inch square baking pan. **Serves 8 to 10.**

*½ cup butter*

*½ cup sugar*

*¾ cup molasses* or ghur *syrup*

*substitute for 1 egg*

*2 cups whole wheat pastry flour*

*1½ tsp baking soda (scant)*

*1 tsp cinnamon*

*1½ tsp powdered ginger*

*½ tsp cloves*

*¾ cup hot water*

*Optional: ⅓ cup finely cut candied ginger or chopped raisins*

In a large bowl, cream together the butter and sugar. Beat in the molasses and egg substitute until the mixture is light and creamy.

Sift the flour and baking soda together in a separate bowl. Stir in the spices. Add one third of the dry mixture into the creamed mixture and beat. Add some of the hot water and beat again. Continue adding the dry mixture and the water, beating between additions, until you have a batter that is fully mixed and fairly wet.

Pour the batter into your prepared pan and bake for approximately 25–30 minutes or until a toothpick inserted into the centre comes out clean.

Cool on a wire rack for 10 to 15 minutes, then remove from the pan and continue to cool. When the gingerbread has cooled, you may drizzle it with the glaze of your choice, dust lightly with icing sugar or serve as is. Store in an airtight container.

# Lemon Cake

This light and delicious cake is easy to make and works like a charm every time. Bake in a preheated medium oven in a greased and floured 9-inch round cake pan. **Serves 8.**

½ cup oil

1¼ cups curd or yogurt

1 tsp vanilla extract

2 tsp lemon zest

1½ cups whole wheat pastry flour

1½ tsp baking powder

½ tsp baking soda

1 cup sugar

Place the oil, yogurt, vanilla and zest together in a large bowl and whisk or beat for a minute or two—until well-mixed.

In another bowl, sift the flour, baking powder and baking soda together. Stir in the sugar. Stir the dry ingredients into the wet and mix briefly, until everything is combined.

Pour the batter into the prepared cake pan and bake for 25–30 minutes or until a cake tester comes out dry.

Rest on a cooling rack for 10 minutes before turning out of the pan. Cool completely before icing.

Serve with a simple lemon glaze or try a buttery lemon icing, as shown in the picture, for a richer version.

# Grandma Anna's Applesauce Crumble Cake

A family favourite, this recipe falls somewhere between a crisp, a cake and a square. It is an excellent recipe for serving a large group, as it may be cut into many small pieces. Vanilla ice cream or a dollop of whipped cream or custard makes a delicious accompaniment. Bake in a preheated medium oven in a greased 14 x 10-inch baking pan.
**Serves 10 to 12.**

*3 cups whole wheat pastry flour*

*2 pinches baking powder*

*1 cup butter*

*1½ cups sugar*

*substitute for 1 egg*

*1 T water*

*1 tsp vanilla*

*1 tsp cinnamon*

*3 cups lightly sweetened applesauce*

In a large bowl, sift the flour and baking powder. Add the butter, sugar, egg substitute, water, vanilla and cinnamon. Using a pastry cutter or your fingertips, work the ingredients until they have a crumble consistency. Press half the mixture into the bottom of your baking pan.

Spread the applesauce evenly over the crumble mixture. Sprinkle the rest of the crumble mixture over the applesauce and pat it down, without pressing too firmly.

Bake until golden brown, approximately 20 minutes. Cool completely in the pan, then cut into squares of whatever size you like.

If you wish to bake a smaller version of this cake, reduce the ingredients by one third and bake in a 9-inch square pan.

# Honey Cake

The flavour of honey is uniquely delicious in cakes and creates a texture that is moist, slightly dense and irresistible. Bake in a preheated slow to medium oven in a greased and floured 9-inch round cake pan. **Serves 8 to 10.**

*1½ tsp instant coffee*

*6 T hot water*

*substitute for 2 eggs*

*½ cup sugar*

*½ cup honey*

*⅓ cup oil*

*1½ cups whole wheat pastry flour*

*1 tsp baking powder*

*½ tsp baking soda*

*½ tsp cinnamon*

*¼ tsp ginger powder*

*a pinch of cloves*

*½ cup finely chopped walnuts (reserve 2 T)*

In a small bowl, dissolve the coffee in the hot water and set aside to cool.

In a large bowl, beat the egg substitute with the sugar, honey and oil until the mixture is light and creamy.

In another bowl, sift the flour with the baking powder and baking soda. Stir in the spices.

Mix one third of the dry ingredients into the bowl of the sugar, honey and oil mixture, then mix in a bit of the coffee and stir. Continue adding the dry ingredients and the coffee into the large bowl, stirring between each addition. Finally, stir in all the walnuts except the 2 T.

Spoon the batter into your prepared cake pan. Sprinkle the remaining walnuts on top and bake for approximately 40 minutes. Cool the cake pan on a rack for about 10 minutes, then remove from the pan and continue to cool.

# Teatime Recipes

# Afternoon Tea

I have a fascination with the tradition of English afternoon tea—perhaps the result of reading Jane Austen over and over again. The kind of baked goods that are served at an English cream tea create a sense of delight and anticipation; it seems like such a romantic meal.

Some years ago, my husband and I had an eleven-hour stopover in London, so we headed downtown to the Covent Garden area. We decided to check out all the hotels and restaurants in the area to see who served afternoon tea. At that time, I'd only read about this culinary ritual and was determined to have the direct experience. We went in and out of many places, including the very posh Savoy Hotel, where, in those days, Sunday Afternoon Tea was twenty-five pounds a person and included ballroom dancing! We settled on a little hotel called the Mountbatten. All my expectations were fulfilled. Pots of steaming, fragrant Darjeeling tea arrived at our table, along with a four-tiered silver serving dish. There were scones served with double Devon cream and little pots of strawberry jam, cucumber sandwiches, with the crusts cut off, as well as many delicate little pastries. We ate and sipped and watched the London world go by. Now I have a lingering desire to do it all over again in the Lake District of England, sitting on a bright green, rolling lawn—or perhaps in Darjeeling, where the tea itself comes from.

The following recipes are all suitable for brunch or an afternoon tea, but of course would be delicious on any occasion.

# Fruit Loaf

This is a delightful recipe, simple and light—just perfect for brunch, an afternoon tea party or a lunch-box treat. Bake in a preheated medium oven in a greased and floured loaf pan or a 9-inch square pan.
**Serves 8.**

⅓ cup oil

¾ cup sugar

1 cup warm (not hot) water

⅓ cup cut raisins

⅓ cup cut dates

⅓ cup chopped walnuts

2 cups whole wheat pastry flour

1 tsp baking soda

1 tsp cinnamon

½ tsp nutmeg

⅛ tsp cloves

In a large bowl, mix the oil and sugar, beating for a minute or two with a wooden spoon. Stir in the water, fruit and nuts.

In another bowl, sift the flour and baking soda and stir in the spices. Mix the dry ingredients into the wet, stirring gently until the batter is fully mixed.

Pour the batter into your prepared baking pan and bake for 30–35 minutes, or until a toothpick inserted into the centre comes out clean.

Cool on a wire rack. After 10 minutes, remove from the pan and continue to cool. This loaf may be served on its own or with butter, jam or a soft cheese such as ricotta or cream cheese. A dusting of icing sugar also gives an elegant finishing touch.

# Cornmeal Biscuits

These light yet satisfying biscuits are a good accompaniment to a meal, or they may be served with cream, jam or honey at brunch or tea. Bake in a preheated hot oven on an ungreased cookie sheet. **Makes 16 biscuits.**

*1¼ cups whole wheat
  pastry flour*

*½ cup cornmeal*
  **(makhi atta)**

*2½ tsp baking powder*

*⅓ cup butter*

*¾ cup milk*

*extra corn meal for
  sprinkling on top*

*optional: ½ tsp mustard
  powder and 1 tsp dill*

Sift the flour and cornmeal together into a large bowl, along with the baking powder. Cut the butter into the flour mixture with a pastry cutter or two knives, until the butter is the size of small crumbs. Add the milk and mix quickly, until the ingredients cling together. Form into a ball and knead gently, folding 8 or 10 times.

On a lightly floured surface, roll the dough to a ½-inch thickness. Cut into rounds with a 2½-inch cookie cutter, or a glass. Sprinkle a pinch of cornmeal on top of each round. Place on your cookie sheet and bake until well-risen and browned on the bottom, about 12–15 minutes. Remove to a cooling rack. These are best baked just before serving, but are still excellent even when baked earlier in the day. While still slightly warm, they may be placed in a basket or bowl lined with a clean cloth.

*(Pictured left on opposite page)*

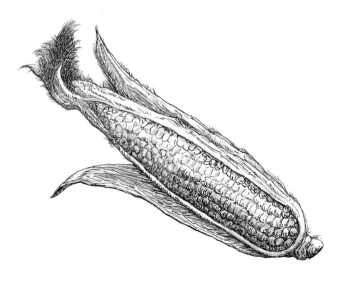

# Raisin Tea Biscuits

These English tea biscuits are also known as Rock Cakes. They are slightly sweet and very satisfying—best eaten the same day they are baked, when the texture is fresh and crumbly. Bake in a preheated medium-hot oven on a lightly greased cookie sheet. **Makes 18 biscuits.**

*2 cups whole wheat
  pastry flour*

*2 tsp baking powder*

*¼ tsp cinnamon*

*½ cup butter*

*⅓ cup sugar*

*1 cup raisins or currants*

*2 T mixed candied
  fruit peel or glacéd
  fruit, if available*

*substitute for 1 egg*

*½ cup milk*

*1 T castor sugar*

Sift the flour and baking powder into a large bowl and add the cinnamon. Rub in the butter until it has the consistency of coarse cornmeal. Mix in the sugar and fruit, then stir in the egg substitute and enough milk to make a dough that has a moist but firm consistency.

For each biscuit, place 2 level tablespoons of dough on the cookie sheet, leaving 2 inches between biscuits. Sprinkle each with a bit of the extra sugar. Bake for about 15 minutes or until light golden-brown. Loosen and transfer to a cooling rack and let cool before serving or storing.

# Biscuits or Shortcake Dough

This is a versatile recipe that can be used in desserts or for a lunch or dinner item. These biscuits are similar to scones. Bake in a preheated hot oven on an ungreased baking tray. **Makes 12 biscuits.**

*1 cup white flour*

*1 cup whole wheat pastry flour*

*2½ tsp baking powder*

*(1 T sugar, optional)*

*¼ cup butter*

*¾ to 1 cup milk or cream*

In a large bowl, sift the flour with the baking powder. If the biscuits are for a dessert, add the tablespoon of sugar. Cut in the butter and mix lightly with your fingertips until the mixture is a fine crumble.

Gradually add the milk or cream (or a combination of the two) and mix lightly with a fork. Using one hand, begin to bring the ingredients together. When the dough comes together into a ball, knead it lightly for barely a half minute. If there is flour in the bowl that does not easily come together, you may add a few more drops of milk. Avoid overworking the dough, as this will create a tougher biscuit.

Roll the dough out to ¾-inch thickness on a lightly floured surface. It may help to flour your rolling pin. Cut the biscuits into 2½- or 3-inch rounds and place on an ungreased baking sheet. Bake for 10–12 minutes or until golden on top.

Transfer to a cooling rack for a few minutes, then wrap in a clean cotton cloth until ready to serve.

# Banana Muffins

These muffins are light, nutritious and very quick to make. They are delicious plain, or spread with butter, jam or honey. Bake in a preheated medium oven in a lightly greased muffin tin. **Makes 12 muffins.**

*¼ cup oil*

*¼ cup light brown sugar*

*¾ cup ripe, mashed bananas*

*½ cup milk*

*1 T apple cider vinegar*

*1 tsp vanilla*

*1 cup whole wheat pastry flour*

*1 tsp baking powder*

*1 scant tsp baking soda*

*1 cup oats*

*¼ tsp nutmeg*

*½ cup cut raisins and/or dates*

In a bowl, stir together the oil and sugar. Mix in the mashed bananas and the liquid ingredients and set aside. In a larger bowl, sift together the flour, baking powder and baking soda. Mix in the oats, nutmeg, raisins and dates.

Make a well in the centre of the dry ingredients and pour all of the wet mixture into it. Mix gently but quickly, so that the dry ingredients are all moistened and integrated, but don't overmix. Spoon the batter into the muffin tin and bake for approximately 15 minutes or until the muffins rise and the top springs back when lightly pressed with your finger.

Let the muffins cool on a rack for a few minutes then gently loosen them with a butter knife and lift from the muffin tin to continue cooling on the rack. They can be enjoyed warm or at room temperature.

# Buttermilk Biscuits

In this variation on the theme of biscuits, buttermilk is the ingredient that yields a very light biscuit. Bake in a preheated hot oven on an ungreased baking tray. **Makes 12 biscuits.**

*1 cup white flour*

*1 cup whole wheat pastry flour*

*2½ tsp baking powder*

*6 T butter*

*¾ to 1 cup buttermilk (or half milk/half yogurt or curd)*

*2 T sugar optional*

In a large bowl, sift the flour together with the baking powder. Cut in the butter until it is the size of small crumbs. If you are using the biscuits for a dessert, stir in the sugar.

Stir in the buttermilk until the ingredients form a ball, and knead very briefly. On a lightly floured surface, roll the dough out to a ¾-inch thickness. Cut into 2½- or 3-inch rounds and bake for approximately 10–12 minutes or until golden on top.

Transfer to a cooling rack for a few minutes, then wrap in a clean cloth until ready to serve.

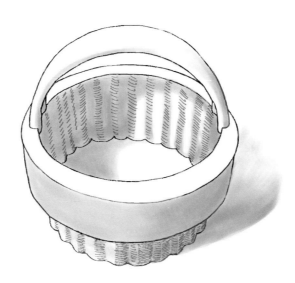

# Date & Nut Cake

This recipe was one of my childhood favourites. My grandmother baked it in large orange juice or coffee cans. When perfectly baked, she would slice it into lovely thin rounds and serve covered with cream cheese. This recipe is unique: it contains no fat whatsoever, yet the cake remains moist and fresh for several days. Bake in a preheated medium oven in a greased and floured 10-inch tube pan. **Serves 10 to 12.**

*1 cup walnut pieces*

*1 cup chopped dates*

*1½ cups sugar*

*2 tsp baking soda*

*1½ cups boiling water*

*substitute for 2 eggs*

*3 cups whole wheat*
  *pastry flour*

*Optional:*

*1 tsp cinnamon*

*½ tsp nutmeg*

*¼ tsp cloves*

Place the walnuts, dates, sugar and baking soda in a large bowl and add the boiling water. Allow to sit for at least thirty minutes. In a separate bowl, sift the flour.

Add the egg substitute to the wet ingredients and stir. Add the flour, one cup at a time, stirring after each addition until just mixed. Pour this batter into your prepared pan and bake for approximately 40 minutes or until a toothpick or cake-tester comes out clean.

Remove from the pan after 10 minutes and cool on a rack. This cake is delicious served plain or with butter or cream cheese. For a fancier presentation you may top with an orange or lemon glaze, or simply dust with icing sugar.

# Lemon Zucchini Bars

This is a healthy and light little cake that will put to use the abundance of zucchini available in the summer. Bake in a preheated medium oven in a greased and floured 9-inch square baking pan or in a muffin tin.
**Makes 16 bars or 12 muffins.**

*2 cups whole wheat
  pastry flour*

*1 tsp baking soda*

*1 cup sugar*

*1 cup yogurt or curd*

*¼ cup melted butter*

*1 T lemon juice*

*1 T grated lemon zest*

*1 cup grated zucchini*

In a large bowl, sift together the flour and baking soda. Stir in the sugar.

In a small bowl, combine the yogurt, melted butter, lemon juice and zest.

Add the wet mixture to the dry and stir until the dry ingredients are just absorbed. Stir in the zucchini and spread the batter into your prepared baking pan. Bake for about 30 minutes, or until a toothpick inserted in the centre comes out clean.

Cool on a rack for 10 minutes, then turn out onto the rack and cool completely before serving. Finish with either a lemon icing or glaze or a dusting of icing sugar. Cut into bars or squares of any size you like.

# Cornbread

This is a delicious quick bread that can be served with breakfast, lunch or dinner, or as an afternoon snack with tea. Bake in a preheated medium oven in a greased and floured 10-inch tube pan or a bread pan. **Serves 8 to 10.**

*1 cup corn flour*
 *(makhi atta)*

*2 cups whole wheat*
 *pastry flour*

*1 T baking powder*

*1 tsp baking soda*

*2 T sugar*

*⅓ cup oil*

*2½ cups yogurt or curd*

Sift the dry ingredients together into a large bowl. Stir in the sugar. In a separate bowl, mix the oil and yogurt together and whisk or beat with a fork.

Make a well in the centre of the dry ingredients, and pour the entire oil and yogurt mixture into it. With a wooden spoon, mix the batter quickly and lightly. Do not overmix.

Pour the batter into your prepared baking pan. Bake for approximately 35 minutes or until a toothpick or cake tester comes out clean. Allow the cornbread to sit in the pan for 10 minutes before turning out onto a cooling rack. Serve with butter, honey or jam.

Optional: If you plan to serve your cornbread as part of a dinner, you can add 1 tsp of dried herbs and ½ tsp mustard powder to the dry ingredients, while reducing the sugar to 1 T.

# Raisin Spice Bars

This very light, tender bar is more like a small cake. It's simple to make and can be served iced, glazed or plain. Bake in a preheated medium oven in a greased and floured 8-inch square pan or a loaf pan. **Makes 16 bars.**

*½ cup brown sugar*

*¼ cup butter*

*¾ cup water*

*½ cup raisins*

*1 tsp cinnamon*

*¼ tsp nutmeg*

*a pinch of cloves*

*½ tsp baking soda*

*2 tsp water*

*1 cup whole wheat
  pastry flour*

*1 tsp baking powder*

*¼ cup chopped walnuts*

Place the sugar, butter, water, raisins and spices in a saucepan and boil for three minutes. Set aside.

In a small bowl, mix the baking soda with the 2 teaspoons of water and stir this into the boiled mixture. Allow to cool. If you're in a hurry, you can cool it more quickly by transferring the mixture into a larger bowl—or divide it into two.

Sift the flour and baking powder into a small bowl. Gently mix this into the wet mixture and spread the batter in your prepared baking pan. Sprinkle the walnuts on top and bake until firm, about 20 minutes.

Cool on a rack for about 10 minutes before removing from the pan. When fully cooled, slice into whatever size you wish.

# Orange Marmalade Biscuits

These are a bit like orange-flavoured scones and are perfect for breakfast or at tea time. Bake in a preheated medium-hot oven on a lightly greased baking sheet. **Makes 18 biscuits.**

*¼ cup butter*

*substitute for 1 egg*

*½ cup orange marmalade*

*½ tsp vanilla extract*

*1 cup whole wheat pastry flour*

*½ tsp baking soda*

*½ tsp baking powder*

*½ tsp cinnamon*

*½ tsp nutmeg*

*½ cup raisins*

*½ cup chopped walnuts*

In a large bowl, cream the butter, mix in the egg substitute, marmalade and vanilla and beat together. In a small bowl, sift together the flour, baking soda and baking powder. Mix the dry ingredients into the wet and beat again. Stir in the spices, the raisins and the walnuts.

Drop batter onto the baking sheet in 1 tablespoon dollops and bake until just starting to turn golden brown, approximately 12–15 minutes.

Cool on the baking sheet for a minute or two and then transfer the biscuits to the cooling rack. These are best eaten the day they are baked.

# Soda Bread

Here is another item that is perfect for the tea table. Serve with jam or honey and butter, or as an accompaniment to a light meal. Mixing dill and a bit of mustard powder into the dough is a nice option if the bread is for a lunch or dinner. Bake in a preheated hot oven on a lightly greased baking sheet. **Serves 8 to 10.**

*2 cups whole wheat
  pastry flour*

*2 cups whole wheat flour*

*1½ tsp baking soda*

*½ cup melted butter*

*1½ cups yogurt, curd
  or buttermilk*

*Optional: Poppy seeds
  or sesame seeds
  sprinkled on top
  of the bread before
  placing in the oven*

Sift the flour and baking soda into a large bowl.

In another bowl, mix together the yogurt and melted butter. Add this to the dry ingredients and using your hand, mix into a moist, slightly sticky dough. Knead it briefly.

Shape the dough into a round, about 9 inches in diameter, and place on your baking sheet. Cut a cross in the top and brush with a little melted butter. Bake for about 40 minutes or until light brown. Cool on a rack. Best served the same day it is made.

# Cookies & Squares

# Cookies

In the U.S. and Canada, these small delights are called cookies. Throughout the rest of the Commonwealth the same items are generally referred to as biscuits, while in North America a biscuit is similar to a scone. Whatever you call them, cookies are enjoyed all over the world, with as many types as there are cultures and cuisines. And there are cookies for so many special days—every major holiday seems to have a cookie of its own to help celebrate the occasion. This book contains several of my favourite cookie recipes for your enjoyment.

Here I would like to mention a few methods of making cookies, and give some hints for their preparation. Once you've mastered these basic techniques any cookie will be easy to make.

Most cookie recipes call for butter and sugar. Many recipes begin by creaming the sugar into the butter. This means your butter should be quite soft, but NOT MELTED. The texture of the cookie will be completely different if you melt the butter. You can use a strong wooden spoon or an electric beater or mixer to cream the butter and sugar. You can also use a food processor, but there is a danger of over mixing in a food processor when adding the flour and other wet ingredients. Each recipe will give you complete instructions.

The simplest type of cookie is the "drop" variety. This means you make your dough and just push a small amount from a spoon onto the cookie sheet. No shaping or rolling is required. When it starts to bake, this type of cookie spreads out and flattens quite a lot, so it is important to leave the space recommended between the cookies or you'll end up with all of them running into each other.

Another type is the shaped cookie. Here, the dough is generally a bit stiffer and you shape it with your hands—into balls or crescents or whatever shape you desire. Akin to this are rolled cookies. This is the type you see as lovely Christmas cookies, with stars and trees and angels—there are all kinds of interesting possibilities. Most kitchen stores sell a selection of cookie cutters, but there's no need to save them for just once a year. Children love to help make this type of cookie and end up not only with a delicious treat, but a host of wonderful memories.

Finally, there are the really fancy cookies, the kind that are not only shaped or cut but are filled with all manner of delicious mixtures. No doubt, these require a bit more effort to make, but they really have a "wow factor." These include sandwich cookies, turnovers, filled thumbprint cookies and cookies that are iced or glazed.

# *Squares*

Squares, or slices as they are known in many places, are a quick and delicious way to get two dozen or more individual-sized treats. The dough for most squares is a lot like cookie dough, but it is pressed into a pan with your fingertips and sliced into pieces after baking. Each recipe specifies when to slice the squares and whether to remove from the pan when totally cooled or still a bit warm. Brownies are the best known squares, but there are many delicious and varied recipes to choose from.

# Oatmeal Coconut Cookies

This delicious, chewy cookie, with the health benefits of oats and coconut, hails from "down under"—a treat from Australia and New Zealand. Bake in a preheated medium oven on a lightly greased cookie sheet. **Makes 24 cookies.**

*1¼ cups white flour*

*¾ cup sugar*

*1¼ cups flaked or desiccated coconut*

*1¼ cups quick cooking oats*

*½ cup plus 2 T butter (125 grams)*

*⅓ cup golden syrup or honey*

*½ tsp baking soda*

*1 T hot water*

In a large bowl, sift the flour and stir in the sugar. Mix in the coconut and the oats and set aside.

In a small saucepan, combine the butter and golden syrup or honey and stir over low heat until the butter is melted. In a small bowl, dissolve the baking soda into the hot water and stir this into the butter mixture (it will foam up). Add this to the dry ingredients and stir until well mixed.

Form into 24 balls and place on the cookie sheet, approximately two inches apart. Flatten the balls slightly with your palm. Bake until they are just golden brown, approximately 10 minutes. Place the baking sheet on a wire rack and cool for a few minutes before transferring the cookies to the rack. Cool completely and store in an airtight container.

# Chocolate Dipped Chocolate Coconut Cookies

For those who love chocolate and coconut, this is a truly delicious choice. Bake in a preheated medium oven on a lightly greased cookie sheet. **Makes 24 cookies.**

*½ cup plus 2 T butter (125 grams)*

*⅔ cup sugar*

*1 tsp vanilla extract*

*substitute for 1 egg*

*scant 1¾ cups whole wheat pastry flour*

*½ tsp baking powder*

*⅓ cup cocoa powder*

*⅔ cup flaked or desiccated coconut*

*⅓ cup chopped dark chocolate or chocolate chips for melting*

*2 T butter*

In a small saucepan, melt the butter and let it cool slightly. In a large bowl, combine the sugar with the vanilla and egg substitute. Pour the melted butter into the sugar mixture and mix together well.

In a separate bowl, sift the flour, baking powder and cocoa powder together. Mix in the coconut and add these ingredients to the butter mixture, again mixing well. Using about 1 tablespoon of dough per cookie, roll into balls.

Place on the cookie sheet, flattening slightly and leaving at least 1 inch between cookies. Bake until just firm, or about 12 minutes. Remove to a cooling rack and when totally cool, dip the tops in melted chocolate. When the chocolate hardens, store the cookies in an airtight container.

To melt the chocolate: in a small saucepan melt the two tablespoons of butter, then stir in the chocolate and keep stirring over a low flame until the mixture is smooth.

# Chocolate-Chip Cookies

These classic cookies are sure to delight your family and friends. They are perfect with a glass of cold milk for the children and a good cup of coffee for you! Bake in a preheated medium oven on a lightly greased cookie sheet. **Makes 36 cookies.**

*1 cup butter*

*¾ cup brown sugar*

*¾ cup sugar*

*1 tsp vanilla*

*substitute for 2 eggs*

*1 cup whole wheat pastry flour*

*1¼ cups white flour*

*1 tsp baking soda*

*1½ cups chocolate chips*

In a large bowl, beat the butter and sugar together until light and creamy. Add the vanilla and egg substitute and beat again. In a separate bowl, sift the flour and baking soda. Gradually add the dry ingredients to the butter mixture, mixing after each addition. Add the chocolate chips and mix again, making sure they are evenly distributed.

Spoon approximately 2 teaspoons of the batter onto your baking sheet and press down slightly. Leave 2 inches between each cookie.

Bake until the edges begin to turn golden brown, approximately 8–10 minutes. Cool slightly and then transfer to a wire rack. Cool completely before storing in an airtight container.

*(Pictured left on opposite page)*

# Peanut Butter Chocolate-Chip Cookies

These cookies are an age-old favourite with adults and children alike. Bake in a preheated medium oven on a lightly greased cookie sheet. **Makes 24 large or 36 small cookies.**

½ cup butter

½ cup brown sugar

½ cup white sugar

substitute for 1 egg

½ teaspoon vanilla

½ cup smooth
 peanut butter

1½ cups white flour

½ tsp baking soda

¾ cup chocolate chips

In a large bowl, cream together the butter and sugar. Beat in the egg substitute, vanilla and peanut butter. In a separate bowl, sift the flour and baking soda. Mix the dry ingredients into the butter and sugar mixture. You may use an electric mixer, a wooden spoon, or even your hands for this. Add the chocolate chips and mix them evenly into the batter.

Using approximately one tablespoon of dough per cookie, form balls and place them 2 inches apart on the cookie sheet. Press each ball with a fork, making the ridges that are this cookie's signature.

Bake until just golden, approximately 8–10 minutes. It's important not to overbake these delicious cookies, so watch them carefully. Cool on the tray for a minute or two before removing to a rack to cool completely. Stored in an airtight container, these cookies keep nicely for several days—if there aren't too many visits to the container!

# Rolled Cookies

These cookies are a delight to make and delicious to eat. Many people collect cookie cutters of all shapes and sizes. Kitchen specialty shops stock all the classics—like hearts, stars and Christmas trees—but these days there are many unique and whimsical choices. Bake in a preheated medium-hot oven on a lightly greased cookie sheet. **Makes 36 cookies.**

½ cup butter

¾ cup sugar

substitute for 2 eggs

1 tsp vanilla extract

1 cup white flour

1½ cups whole wheat
  pastry flour

1½ tsp baking powder

In a large bowl, use an electric mixer or a wooden spoon to cream the butter and sugar together until light and creamy. Mix in the egg substitute and vanilla and beat well.

In a separate bowl, sift the dry ingredients. Slowly add the dry ingredients into the wet, mixing between each addition. Alternatively, you can pulse all the ingredients in a food processor, being careful not to overdo it.

Chill the dough for about one hour before rolling it out on a lightly floured surface (a marble counter or slab works well). The dough should be approximately ⅛-inch thick. Use your cookie cutters or a glass to cut out shapes.

Place one inch apart on a lightly greased baking sheet and bake for 7–10 minutes, or until the edges of the cookies turn golden brown. Remove from the cookie sheet to a cooling rack. When the cookies are completely cool store in an airtight container. They may be decorated with icing and sprinkles.

# Brownies

This recipe is easy to make and really delicious—moist and chewy, just the way brownies should be. Serve with vanilla ice cream for a crowd-pleasing dessert. Bake in a preheated medium oven in a lightly greased and floured 9-inch square pan. **Makes 16 large or 24 small brownies.**

¾ cup butter

½ cup cocoa powder

substitute for 3 eggs

1 tsp vanilla

1¼ cups whole wheat
   pastry flour

a pinch of baking
   powder

1½ cups sugar

¾ cup walnuts

Melt the butter and cocoa powder together over low heat. Set aside to cool. Prepare the egg substitute and set aside.

In a large bowl, sift the flour and baking powder, and stir in the sugar and walnuts.

Next, stir the egg substitute and vanilla into the cooled butter and cocoa mixture and pour this into the dry ingredients. Stir all together until just blended; don't overmix this batter.

Spoon into your prepared pan and spread evenly. Bake until the top is just firm and a bit crinkly looking, and the edges begin to pull away from the sides of the pan, approximately 20 minutes. Cool fully in the pan before cutting. This is really important—if you try to cut or remove brownies from the pan while still warm, they will crumble and fall apart.

For a richer dessert these may be iced. They also look festive with a light sifting of icing sugar on top.

*(Pictured left on opposite page)*

# Peanut Butter Blondies

This is a rich and sophisticated square that will be very popular with those who love chocolate and peanut butter. Bake in a preheated medium-hot oven in a greased and floured 8-inch square pan. **Makes 16 squares.**

¼ cup butter

½ cup brown sugar

½ cup sugar

substitute for 3 eggs

1 tsp vanilla extract

½ cup smooth
 peanut butter

1 cup whole wheat
 pastry flour

¼ tsp baking powder

⅛ tsp baking soda

¾ cup dark
 chocolate chips

In a large mixing bowl, cream the butter and sugar. Add the egg substitute and vanilla, then the peanut butter, beating well after each addition.

In another bowl, sift the flour together with the baking powder and baking soda. Slowly add the dry ingredients to the wet, and beat or stir until well mixed. Stir in the chocolate chips. Transfer the batter to your prepared baking pan, and smooth with a spatula.

Bake for about 20 minutes or until golden. The squares should start to pull away from the sides of the pan. Cool on a wire rack and slice in the pan when completely cool. If you try to cut while still hot, the squares will crumble and fall apart. These keep fresh for several days stored in an airtight container.

# Amazing Squares

These squares are quick, easy and utterly delicious! They are rich, sweet and have a party air about them. Bake in a preheated medium oven in a well-greased 9-inch square baking pan. **Makes 36 small squares.**

*½ cup melted butter*

*1 cup whole wheat pastry flour*

*1 tsp baking powder*

*¾ cup sugar*

*1½ cups chocolate chips*

*1 cup flaked or desiccated coconut*

*1 cup chopped walnuts*

*1 400-gram can sweetened condensed milk*

Combine the melted butter, flour, baking powder and sugar in a bowl, rubbing them together until uniformly blended. Press this mixture into the baking pan.

Sprinkle the chocolate chips over the base, then the coconut, distributing evenly. Top with the walnuts and pour the entire can of milk evenly over it all.

Bake for approximately 25 minutes, or until the milky topping starts firming up in the centre. The outside edges may become quite browned—this is perfectly fine.

Place the pan on a wire rack and cut into squares when cool. Remove squares from the pan and cool completely before serving or packing in an airtight container.

# Chocolate-Chip Coffee Squares

These squares can be made with real coffee or with coffee substitute. Bake in a preheated medium oven in a lightly greased 9-inch square pan. Rich and delicious, they may be cut very small. **Makes 24 or 36 squares.**

*1 cup butter*

*½ cup brown sugar*

*½ cup sugar*

*1 tsp vanilla*

*1 T instant coffee dissolved in 2 T warm water*

*2 cups whole wheat pastry flour*

*½ tsp baking powder*

*1 cup chocolate chips*

In a large bowl, beat the butter and sugar together until light and creamy. Beat in the vanilla and coffee.

In a separate bowl, sift the flour with the baking powder.

Slowly add the flour and baking powder to the butter and sugar in two or three stages, beating well after each addition. Add the chocolate chips and beat again until well mixed.

Pat the dough into your prepared pan and bake until just firm and starting to turn a golden colour, about 20 minutes. The squares may seem a bit underbaked but will firm up when cool. Cool for at least 10 minutes before cutting and removing from the pan, then cool the squares completely on a wire rack before storing in an airtight container. These will keep for several days.

# Holiday Cookies

Easy to make and delicious to eat, these cookies are the very essence of holiday baking. Bake in a preheated medium oven on a lightly greased cookie sheet. **Makes 24 cookies.**

¾ *cup butter*

*1 cup sugar*

*substitute for 1 egg*

*1 tsp vanilla extract*

*1¼ cups white flour*

*½ tsp baking soda*

*1 cup chopped pecans or walnuts*

*1 cup chocolate chips*

*1 cup coconut powder*

*1 cup mixed candied fruit*

*⅓ cup chopped candied ginger*

In a large bowl, cream together the butter and sugar. Add the egg substitute and vanilla, and beat.

In a smaller bowl, sift the flour and baking soda together. Beat this into the large bowl of wet ingredients.

Add all the remaining ingredients into the bowl and mix well. The batter will be a bit stiff and dry. If needed, you can add a couple of teaspoons of water.

Drop approximately 2 teaspoons of batter onto the cookie sheet leaving 2 inches between each cookie. Bake for 12–15 minutes or until golden.

Cool the baking sheet on a rack for a couple of minutes, then transfer the cookies onto the rack to continue cooling. When cool, store in an airtight container.

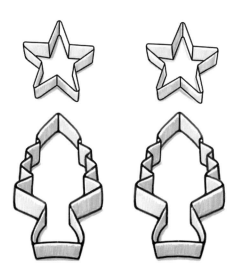

# Oatmeal Raisin Chocolate-Chip Cookies

The oats and raisins in these delicious cookies make you feel like they are almost a health food! Bake in a preheated medium-hot oven on a lightly greased cookie sheet. **Makes 24 cookies.**

*½ cup butter*

*1 cup sugar*

*substitute for 1 egg*

*1 T water*

*1 tsp vanilla extract*

*¾ cup whole wheat pastry flour*

*½ tsp baking soda*

*1½ cups quick cooking oats*

*½ cup raisins*

*½ cup chocolate chips*

In a large bowl, cream together the butter and sugar. Beat in the egg substitute, water and vanilla. In another bowl, sift the flour and baking soda together and stir in the oats.

Mix the dry ingredients gradually into the butter mixture, beating between additions. Add the raisins and chocolate chips and beat until evenly distributed.

Drop approximately 1 tablespoon of dough onto the cookie sheet about 2 inches apart, and bake for 8–10 minutes, or until the edges begin to brown lightly. Cool trays on a wire rack for a couple of minutes before lifting the cookies onto the rack for complete cooling. These are delicious eaten while slightly warm, and keep nicely for several days in an airtight container.

# Cream Cheese Crescents (Ruggelach)

These little crescents are very elegant and rich, but not overly sweet. Don't be intimidated—they really aren't difficult to make, and once you've tasted them they will become one of your showcase recipes. Bake in a preheated medium-hot oven on an ungreased cookie sheet.
**Makes 32 crescents.**

*1 cup soft butter*

*¾ cup sugar*

*1 cup cottage cheese or cream cheese or ricotta or finely crumbled paneer*

*2 cups white flour*

*Fillings: chocolate spread, such as Nutella, or jam or finely chopped walnuts mixed with cinnamon and sugar*

Place butter, sugar, cheese and flour in a bowl and mix thoroughly, either with your hands or in a food processor. Divide the dough into four even-sized balls and chill, covered in the refrigerator for about an hour. On a lightly floured board or marble counter, roll one ball out into an approximately 9-inch circle. Sprinkle with the cinnamon and nut mixture, or spread any other filling of your choice onto the surface, being careful not to tear the dough.

Using a knife or a pizza cutter, score the circle into 8 sections. Roll each section gently from the outside to the centre point. Lift one by one onto the baking sheet, leaving 2 inches between each cookie. Slightly bend each piece to form a crescent shape. Repeat until all 32 pieces are ready, and bake until the edges begin to lightly brown, approximately 12 minutes. Cool for a few minutes and then transfer to a wire rack. Cool completely before serving or storing in an airtight container.

Note: Depending upon your choice of cheese, the result will differ slightly, but any of the cheeses listed will yield a very delicious treat.

# Chocolate Butter Cookies

These cookies are light and very subtle. They may be made as is, or "fancied up" with fillings of various kinds. Bake in a preheated medium oven on a lightly greased cookie sheet. **Makes 24 cookies.**

*¾ cup butter*

*½ cup sugar*

*substitute for 1 egg*

*1 tsp almond extract*

*¾ cup white flour*

*¾ cup whole wheat pastry flour*

*¼ cup cocoa powder*

In a large bowl, combine the butter, sugar, egg substitute and almond extract. Beat well until mixed and creamy.

In another bowl, sift together the flour and cocoa and add gradually to the butter mixture, beating or stirring until well mixed.

Shape as desired. You may make balls, round cookies or fingers. At this point, you can decide if you want your cookies filled, glazed or dipped in melted chocolate. They are also excellent plain, and are best when not pressed too flat.

Place cookies on the prepared baking sheet 2 inches apart and bake for 8–10 minutes. Allow the cookies to cool for a minute or two on the baking sheet before transferring to a cooling rack.

To make the classic filled "thumbprint" cookie, make an indentation in the centre of each cookie about half-way through baking. When the cookies are cool, using a small spoon, fill the indentation with your choice of jam, melted chocolate or a firm icing.

# European Walnut Crescents

These can be shaped as crescents or made as a simple, round cookie. They are very rich and very delicious—perfect with a cup of coffee. Bake in a preheated medium oven on an ungreased cookie sheet. **Makes 36 crescents.**

*2 cups white flour*

*1 cup soft butter*

*1 cup icing sugar*

*1 cup finely chopped walnuts*

*1 tsp vanilla or almond extract*

Place all the ingredients in a large bowl and mix thoroughly with your hands or in a food processor until you have a smooth, uniform dough. Form it into a ball and knead for half a minute.

Break off walnut-sized pieces and shape as you wish. To make the crescent, firm the piece of dough in your hand and roll it back and forth on a board or counter until you have a 4-inch roll. Shape each roll into a crescent and place on the cookie sheet, approximately 2 inches apart.

Bake until the cookies are a light golden colour, about 8–10 minutes. Do not let them brown or overbake. Cool for a minute or two and transfer to a wire rack until completely cooled. These versatile cookies keep well for up to one week when stored in an airtight container.

# Orange Chocolate-Chip Shortbread

Chocolate and orange is an unbeatable combination, and the taste of fresh orange zest is irresistible in this rich, buttery cookie. Bake in a preheated hot oven on an ungreased cookie sheet. **Makes 32 shortbreads.**

*1 cup soft butter*

*1 cup sifted icing sugar*

*2 cups white flour*

*1 T grated orange zest*

*¾ cup chocolate chips*

Place all the ingredients in a bowl and mix fully, using your hands or a food processor. Form the dough into four balls of even size. On your cookie sheet, press one of the balls of dough into a circle approximately 7 inches in diameter and ¼-inch thick. Use your finger tips to shape it nicely. If there is room on the cookie sheet for another ball, repeat the process. There should be at least 2 inches between the circles of dough. Prick the dough here and there with a fork.

Bake for approximately 15–18 minutes, or until the edges begin to turn golden brown. Remove from the oven and after cooling one or two minutes, score the circle into 8 parts with a sharp knife or a pizza cutter. Allow a few minutes more to cool and then remove cookies from the tray and place on a cooling rack. Cool completely before storing in an airtight container. These will keep well for up to one week.

If you want smaller cookies, cut the circle into 12 parts. You may also form the dough into 30 small balls and press them onto an ungreased baking sheet to make round cookies.

Optional: For a fancy version, dip the wide edge of each cookie in melted, dark chocolate. Place on a cooling rack until the chocolate becomes dry and firm before storing the cookies.

# Chocolate-Chip Brownie Cookies

These are great! They are almost as satisfying as brownies, but with a lot less butter, and they have the added benefit of oats. Bake in a preheated medium oven on a lightly greased cookie sheet. **Makes 24 cookies.**

*⅓ cup butter*

*1 cup sugar*

*substitute for 1 egg*

*⅔ cup whole wheat pastry flour*

*1½ tsp baking powder*

*½ cup cocoa powder*

*1 cup quick cooking oats*

*½ cup chocolate chips*

*½ cup chopped walnuts*

*⅓ cup milk*

In a large bowl, cream the butter and sugar together. Add the egg substitute and mix well.

In another bowl, sift flour, baking powder and cocoa powder. Stir in the oats, chocolate chips and walnuts. Gradually add the dry ingredients to the butter and sugar mixture, alternately mixing in the milk. When the batter is well mixed, refrigerate it for about one hour. (If you don't feel like waiting, you can bake them right away, but the dough will be a bit sticky to work with.)

Using two spoons—one to pick up the dough and the other to push it onto the baking tray—pick up approximately 2 teaspoons of batter and drop or push it onto your baking tray, approximately 2 inches apart.

Bake for 10–12 minutes. The cookies will seem very soft, but will firm up as they cool. Place the cookie sheet on a cooling rack for a minute or two, then transfer the cookies to the rack and let them cool completely before storing in an air-tight container.

# Date Squares

Date squares are found in every bakery in North America, where there are as many versions as bakers. If you like oats you may replace ¼ cup of the flour with them. Date squares are naturally sweet and they keep well in the refrigerator. Bake in a preheated medium oven in a lightly greased 9-inch square pan. **Makes 16 squares.**

*2 cups of washed, pitted, chopped dates*

*1 cup water or part orange juice*

*1 tsp vanilla*

*1½ cups whole wheat pastry flour*

*½ cup soft butter*

*¾ cup sugar*

*1 tsp cinnamon*

In a heavy pot, gently boil the dates in the cup of water, covered until they cook down into a thick paste. You may need to add more water or juice before they reach this stage. Be sure to stir them now and then to prevent sticking. When they reach the desired thick, creamy consistency, stir in the vanilla.

In a large bowl, sift the flour. Add the butter, sugar and cinnamon. Work these ingredients with your fingertips (or pulse them in a food processor, being careful not to overprocess them) until you have a crumbly mixture.

Press half the crumble mixture firmly into the bottom of your baking pan, making sure it is evenly distributed. Spread the cooked date mixture evenly over the base. Sprinkle the rest of the crumble mixture on top of the dates, patting it gently into place, but not pressing it down.

Bake for approximately 25 minutes or until the crumble topping turns a deep golden brown. Cool the pan on a rack for at least 15 minutes and then cut into squares. Serve with vanilla ice cream for a real treat.

# Shortbread

This classic recipe is rich and very "short," which means it contains lots of butter. These cookies are perfect with a good cup of tea, and they stay fresh for one week when stored in an airtight container. Bake in a preheated hot oven. **Makes 24 large or 36 small shortbreads.**

*1½ cups soft butter*

*2 cups white flour*

*¾ cup whole wheat pastry flour*

*1⅓ cups sifted icing sugar*

Place all the ingredients in a bowl and mix thoroughly with your hands, eventually kneading into a smooth, uniform dough. A food processor may also be used, but you will still need to knead the dough a turn or two after processing.

Pinch off pieces of dough the size of walnuts and roll into balls. Place on an ungreased cookie sheet, leaving 2 inches between each shortbread. Press each ball of dough with a decorative cookie press or the bottom of a glass that has a nice design on it. You may need to lightly dust the press between applications, using either flour or icing sugar.

Bake for 10–12 minutes or until the edges are golden in colour. Allow the cookies to cool on the baking sheet for a couple of minutes before lifting them onto a cooling rack. Cool completely before storing in an airtight container.

Optional: Grated orange or lemon zest may be added to the dough before mixing. Also, vanilla, maple and almond extracts impart different and lovely tastes to this recipe. Use one teaspoon of extract.

Variations: These cookies may also be made by pressing the dough evenly into a pan that is approximately 9 x 12 inches, with sides that are at least ½ inch high. The dough should be about a ½-inch thick when pressed into the pan. Prick the dough with a fork in several places before placing in the oven and bake until it begins to take on a golden colour, about 20 minutes. While still warm, but not hot, cut into the size and shape of cookie desired. Wait until they are quite cool to remove from the pan.

You may also press the dough into a round pan to make the traditional Scottish shortbread shape, cutting into pie-shaped wedges while still slightly warm.

# Pies & Pastries

# Pies & Pastries

Nothing quite compares with the aroma of a freshly baked fruit pie wafting through your home. And there is nothing as delicious or satisfying to bake and eat! In the summer when fruit is abundant, juicy and ripe, cobblers, crisps, pies and tarts are wonderful dessert choices. A scoop of vanilla ice cream on the side makes your dish "à la mode" and is an extra special treat.

The key to making tender and flaky pastry is to not overwork the dough. With pastry, less is more, which means use as little water as possible when forming the dough. Also avoid using too much extra flour when rolling out the dough. After making your pastry, place it in a bowl and cover with a clean cloth. Place the bowl in the fridge, letting your pastry "rest" for 30 minutes, then roll out according to the recipe.

In all things, practice does make perfect, but really, pastry is not that difficult to master. And the results are very rewarding.

Hint: Use ice cold water and butter when making pastry.

# Peach Pie

Succulent, spiced peaches baked in a meltingly delicious double-crust pastry shell—this peach pie will wow your guests. Bake in a preheated hot oven in a 9-inch pie pan. **Serves six to eight.**

Prepare the pastry recipe on page 90 and have ready to roll out.

*The filling:*

*4 cups fresh ripe peaches*

*2 T cornstarch*

*⅓ cup sugar*

*2 T lemon juice*

*½ tsp cinnamon*

*½ tsp nutmeg*

Wash and peel the peaches. If they are not easy to peel, you can drop them into boiling water for a minute. Remove quickly and transfer into a bowl of cold water. The skins will now slip off easily. If you are using freestone peaches, they can be halved easily and then sliced. If you can't get freestone peaches, slice from the outside towards the centre of each peach and the slices should come off the pit easily.

Place the sliced peaches in a large bowl and add the remaining ingredients. Using a wooden spoon, mix everything together well. Set aside while you prepare the pastry.

Roll out the pastry and place in the pie pan. Pour the peaches into the pan and place the second roll of pastry on the top. Crimp the edges with a fork or your fingers. With a sharp knife, make three or four small cuts in the top crust to allow the steam to escape.

Bake for approximately 40 minutes or until the crust is golden-brown and your kitchen smells heavenly! Allow the pie to cool, either partially or totally, and slice it in the pie pan. Serve on its own or with vanilla ice cream or a dollop of whipped cream.

# Peach Cobbler 1

A cobbler is a fruit dessert that hails from the American South. Sometimes it's made with berries, sometimes with peaches or apricots—either way it's always delicious. You could even make a cobbler with mangos—the fruit just needs to be a juicy variety. Bake in a preheated medium oven in a greased 9-inch round pan. **Serves 6 to 8.**

*The fruit:*

*3 cups sliced peaches*

*2 T cornstarch or white flour*

*2 T lemon juice*

*¼ cup sugar*

*½ tsp cinnamon*

*¼ tsp nutmeg*

*¼ tsp cloves*

*The topping:*

*1 cup flour*

*1 tsp baking powder*

*½ cup sugar*

*½ tsp cinnamon*

*½ tsp nutmeg*

*¾ cup milk*

*¼ cup melted butter*

Prepare the peaches as in the instructions for peach pie. In a large bowl, mix the peaches with the cornstarch, lemon juice, sugar and spices. Place this mixture into your prepared baking pan.

In a separate bowl, sift the flour and baking powder. Stir in the sugar and the spices. Mix the milk and the melted butter into the flour mixture and stir until the ingredients are just mixed.

Spoon the topping over the fruit and spread it about. Don't be concerned if there are small gaps in the topping. It will fill in as it bakes. Bake for approximately 30 minutes or until the topping is golden and the peaches are bubbling up. Serve warm or cold, with vanilla ice cream or a spoonful of heavy cream.

*(Pictured top left on previous page)*

# Peach Cobbler 2

Here is another version of this delicious dessert—try both and see which you prefer. Bake in a preheated medium oven in a 9-inch round baking pan. **Serves 6 to 8.**

*2 cups sliced peaches*

*1 T lemon juice*

*1 T cornstarch or
  white flour*

*3 T sugar*

*¼ cup butter*

*1 cup flour*

*1½ tsp baking powder*

*½ cup sugar*

*½ tsp cinnamon*

*½ tsp nutmeg*

*¾ cup milk or
  buttermilk*

Prepare the peaches as in the previous recipe. Place in a bowl and add the lemon juice, cornstarch and sugar. Mix together and set aside.

Place the butter in your baking pan and set it in your preheated oven to melt. Remove from the oven when the butter is melted (be careful not to let it burn) and set aside.

In a bowl, sift the flour and the baking powder. Stir in the sugar and the spices. Mix in the milk and stir until you have a medium-thick batter.

Pour or spoon the batter directly over the melted butter. Do not stir this. Now place the peaches evenly on top of the batter, again not stirring. Place in the oven and bake for approximately 30 minutes, or until the batter becomes firm, golden brown and rises up here and there around the peaches.

Serve warm or cold, with ice cream or cream.

# Apple Crisp

Whether you call it a crisp or a crumble, this classic dessert is always a hit. This recipe works well with peaches, apricots and many other fruits and may be served on its own, or with vanilla ice cream or a dollop of whipped cream. Bake in a preheated slow to medium oven in a greased 9-inch round baking dish. **Serves approximately 8.**

*6 to 8 medium
sized apples*

*3 T sugar*

*1 to 2 T lemon juice*

*½ tsp cinnamon*

*¼ tsp nutmeg*

*⅛ tsp cloves*

*1½ cups whole wheat
pastry flour*

*½ cup butter*

*¾ cup sugar*

Peel and core the apples and slice them thinly—a food processor may be used for this. In a large bowl, toss the sliced apples with 3 T sugar, the lemon juice and the spices. Place the apples in your baking dish.

In a medium bowl, sift the flour and add the butter and sugar. Work these ingredients together with your fingertips until you have a crumbly mixture. You may add a pinch more cinnamon, nutmeg and clove at this point. Spread this topping over the apples, without pressing it down too firmly.

Bake in a slow oven for the first 15 minutes, then increase to a medium oven and continue to bake until the topping turns golden brown and you see the apples begin to bubble a bit on the sides, approximately another 15–20 minutes. Serve the crisp directly from the baking dish, either warm or at room temperature.

Optional: Replace ½ cup of the flour with ½ cup of quick cooking oats.

# Granola

This granola recipe is easy and delicious. There's nothing quite so satisfying as making your own breakfast cereal. Bake in a preheated medium oven.

*10 cups oats*

*1 cup whole wheat pastry flour*

*1 cup sunflower seeds or* magaz

*1 cup walnuts broken into medium sized pieces*

*1 cup sesame seeds*

*1 cup raisins*

*1 cup oil*

*1 cup honey*

Place all the dry ingredients in a very large bowl. Make a well in the centre and pour in the honey and oil. Mix everything together thoroughly. The easiest way is to just dive in and use your hands.

Spread a third of the granola mixture on a large cookie sheet that has slightly raised sides. Bake until you just begin to smell the granola roasting, approximately 10 minutes. Take the sheet out of the oven and with a heatproof spatula gently scrape the granola from the outsides of the tray towards the centre, stirring to turn it over. Return the tray to the oven and stir again after another 5–7 minutes. You will need to do this around four times, until the granola is a toasty brown, the raisins have plumped up and your house smells wonderful. Repeat until all the ingredients have been baked.

Transfer the granola to a large metal bowl or *paraat* and allow it to cool completely before storing in an airtight container. Once you taste this, you will never want to eat store-bought cereal again! Of course this recipe may be halved to make a smaller amount of granola.

# Pie Dough

This makes an excellent, flaky pie crust. Makes enough dough for a double crust pie.

*1 cup white flour*

*1 cup whole wheat pastry flour*

*⅔ cup cold butter*

*7–8 T cold water*

In a large bowl, sift the flour. Cut in the butter, using two knives or a pastry cutter, until it is the size of small crumbs. Slowly add the water, stirring lightly with one hand or with a fork until the dough clings together. Form into a couple of balls, cover and chill in the fridge for about 30 minutes.

Roll out on a lightly floured surface and lift gently into a pie plate, or for individual servings, into muffin or tart tins.

Hint: For a light, flaky crust, handle the dough as little as possible.

# Strawberry Shortcake

The essence of summer, a simple strawberry shortcake is a vision of elegance and a delicious dessert, or a perfect item for afternoon tea. **Serves 8.**

The shortcake: Prepare and bake either the recipe for biscuits on page 42 or for buttermilk biscuits on page 44, cutting out 8 good size biscuits.

The strawberries: Wash 3 cups of strawberries and drain well. Slice the berries and sprinkle them with 3 tablespoons of sugar, or according to taste. Lightly mash half of the berries and retain the rest in a separate bowl.

If there are concerns about eating uncooked fruit, you may place the strawberries and sugar in a pan and lightly cook for a minute or two. This will create more juice

than you may wish to use. The juice can be drained and saved in the fridge for a few days to use in a drink or as part of another dessert.

The cream: Using an electric hand mixer or a whisk, whip a small container of cream, adding a half teaspoon of vanilla and two tablespoons of fine sugar. Whip only until the cream forms soft peaks. Alternatively, you may use vanilla ice cream or lightly sweetened dripped yogurt.

To assemble: Slice a shortcake open and place on an individual serving plate. Spoon a generous amount of the mashed strawberries over the bottom half of the shortcake. On top of the berries, place an equally generous amount of cream or ice cream. Top the cream with some of the berries that have not been mashed. Lightly place the top of the shortcake over this and serve with a dessert fork.

Serving hint: To assemble this dessert with ease at the end of a dinner, slice the shortcakes open and place on the plates just before dinner. With the whipped cream and strawberries ready in the fridge, it will then be quick and easy to plate up this lovely dessert.

An alternative serving technique is to bake the shortcake into one large round (use an 8-inch cake or pie pan) and carefully slice open. Or if you prefer, bake two thinner rounds. Create a single, large strawberry shortcake and cut as you would a cake.

# Pastries or Turnovers

Pastries are a perfect way to use up left-over pie dough or as an alternative to a pie. Bake in a hot oven on an ungreased baking tray.

Prepare the pie dough recipe on page 90.

Roll pastry out into an 8- or 9-inch circle. Score into 8 sections and place the filling of your choice on each section. You can use chopped nuts and dates, mince filling, jam or whatever you like. Roll each section into a crescent, from the outside edge towards the centre, and place on your baking sheet. Bake for about 15 minutes, or until the pastry begins to turn a lovely golden-brown colour. Remove to a cooling rack and serve the same day.

The same dough may be used to make turnovers. Roll the pastry out and cut into 3- or 4-inch circles. Place a tablespoon of filling on the bottom half of the circle and fold the top half down, creating a half-moon shape, much like *gujiya*. Use a fork to seal the dough, and bake until golden.

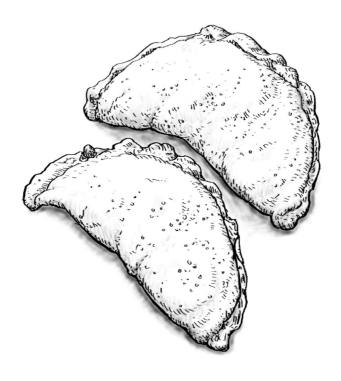

# Mince Tarts

This is a very refreshing mixture. Mince filling works well in a pie or in individual tarts or turnovers. Bake in a preheated hot oven in an ungreased muffin tin or a 9-inch pie pan. Shown here as mini-tarts. **Makes one pie, serving 6 to 8, or 24 mini-tarts.**

*1½ cups cut raisins*

*4 medium apples, peeled and minced*

*grated zest and juice of 1 orange*

*¾ cup sugar*

*½ tsp cinnamon*

*¼ tsp nutmeg*

*⅛ tsp cloves*

*3 T finely crushed cream crackers*

Simmer the raisins, apples, juice and zest together until the apples are soft. Stir in the sugar, spices and cracker crumbs and mix well. This may be refrigerated until you are ready to use it, even one or two days ahead.

Prepare your pastry following the recipe on page 90. Roll it out and place in your choice of baking pan. Spoon the mince filling into the pastry and bake until the edges of the pastry begin to turn an inviting golden-brown colour. Cool for a few minutes on a rack. If you have baked small tarts, remove them from the pan and continue to cool before storing in an air tight container. Pie can be cut and served directly from the pie tin.

# Icings & Glazes

# Icings & Glazes

The crowning glory, the finishing touch, the icing on the cake—these phrases describe the very best or the final stage of any creation. In the field of baking they take on a practical and literal meaning. A simple dusting of icing sugar changes the look of a cake from simple to sophisticated. A beautiful swirled icing has real "wow" factor, and an elegant glaze drizzled over a cake, cookies or squares is truly the finishing touch. Sauces made of fruit or chocolate can be spooned over individual slices of cake, allowing each person to choose how rich or modest his dessert should be. The following recipes offer a variety of choices and may be interchangeably used with any of the desserts.

Hint: For ease in making perfect icing, start with soft butter and always sift the sugar.

# Glazes

Glazes provide a subtle finishing touch to many cakes, cookies or squares. A glaze looks elegant, is flavourful and has the advantage of using much less sugar and butter than a traditional frosting.

*½ cup icing sugar*

*1 T milk*

*1½ tsp soft butter*

*a few drops of any flavoured extract, such as vanilla, almond, or maple*

Sift the icing sugar into a medium bowl. Using a wooden spoon, stir the milk into the icing sugar. Then add the butter and stir well, until the three ingredients have become a smooth paste or glaze. Add your flavouring and stir again. If you would like the glaze to be somewhat more liquid, carefully add a few more drops of milk, juice or water until the desired consistency is reached.

You may drizzle the glaze over your baking, creating a design of fine lines. Or apply the glaze with a knife, smoothing it over the entire cake, tray of squares or the tops of cookies.

Variations to this recipe include substituting lemon juice or orange juice for the milk. A teaspoon of finely grated citrus zest adds a great flavour.

For a vegan glaze, omit the butter and substitute water or juice for the milk.

# Streusel Topping

This is a tasty and sophisticated cake topping, enough for one large cake. It is the traditional topping for coffee cakes, but is delicious on any type of cake at all and goes particularly well with apples.

*½ cup brown sugar*

*¼ cup butter*

*¼ cup white flour*

*1 tsp cinnamon*

Place all the ingredients in a bowl and mix lightly with your fingertips, or pulse briefly in a food processor. The ingredients should only come together enough to form large crumbs. Sprinkle on the top of your cake, either part way through baking or before putting into the oven.

For an interesting variation, you may spoon half your cake batter into your prepared pan, then sprinkle half of the streusel topping over it. Cover with the rest of the cake batter and top with the remaining streusel mixture. Enough for one cake.

# Chocolate Frosting

*1½ cups icing sugar*

*⅓ cup cocoa powder*

*⅓ cup butter*

*2 to 3 T milk*

In a deep bowl, sift the icing sugar and cocoa powder. Add the butter and beat with an electric mixer or by hand with a wooden spoon. Add the milk, gradually beating until the frosting is fluffy and spreadable.

Alternatively, you may place all of the ingredients in a food processor and pulse, then process for a minute. This frosting may be flavoured with almond extract.

Hint: It is important to sift the dry ingredients or you may have a frosting that is grainy or lumpy. Enough for one cake.

# Vanilla Frosting

*1½ cups icing sugar*

*⅓ cup butter*

*2 T milk*

*½ tsp vanilla extract*

Sift the icing sugar and place in a deep bowl. Add the softened butter and slowly begin to beat together with an electric mixer or by hand with a wooden spoon. Drizzle in the milk and keep beating until you get the desired consistency—it should be smooth and spreadable. Add the vanilla extract and beat again. Alternatively, you can place all the ingredients in a food processor and pulse together and then process for a minute.

This recipe also works well with almond or maple extract. Enough for one cake.

# Cream Cheese Icing

This icing is rich, delicious and subtle.

*one eight-ounce packet of cream cheese or one cup of thick dripped yogurt or curd*

*¼ cup (50 grams) soft butter*

*½ tsp vanilla*

*1 cup sifted icing sugar*

Place the cream cheese and butter in a bowl and beat with an electric beater until light and fluffy. Add the vanilla and one third of the icing sugar and beat again. Continue adding the icing sugar and beating until all the ingredients are well mixed and the icing is ready to spread.

This may also be made in a food processor. Enough for one cake.

# Honey-Chocolate Sauce

This delicious sauce is low in fat and calories and is great spooned over a simple cake or on ice-cream.

*⅓ cup sifted cocoa powder*

*¼ cup brown sugar (light or dark)*

*1 T cornstarch*

*½ cup milk (whole or skim)*

*¼ cup honey*

*1 tsp vanilla*

In a medium saucepan, combine the cocoa powder, brown sugar and cornstarch. Mix together and press out any lumps in the sugar or cocoa. Gradually stir in the milk and honey. Bring mixture to a boil, stirring continuously for one minute, or until the sauce thickens. Remove from the heat and stir in the vanilla. Enjoy this tasty sauce hot or cold. It keeps well in the fridge for several days. Enough for one cake.

# Fruit Coulis

This is a lovely and light way to adorn a cake. Fresh fruit, slightly sweetened and silky smooth can be spooned over individual slices of cake, or spread over the entire cake before it is cut.

Use two cups of ripe fruit. Peaches, apricots, strawberries, blackberries, blueberries and raspberries are all good choices. Wash the fruit well and drain it thoroughly. Blend the fruit completely in either a blender or a food processor.

If your choice of fruit contains small seeds, push the fruit pulp through a strainer using the back of a spoon, and dispose of the seeds that are left behind.

Add sifted icing sugar to taste and mix in well. You may add a squeeze of lemon juice if the fruit is very sweet. Spoon the coulis over your dessert and enjoy. Enough for one cake.

# *Glossary*

**Applesauce**—a puree of cooked apples that are lightly sweetened and seasoned with lemon and cinnamon.

**Aromatic Spices:**

**Cinnamon**—(Hindi: *dalchini*) cinnamon is a bark which is commonly ground into a powder for use in baking.

**Cloves**—(Hindi: *laung*) cloves are ground into powder for baking and used sparingly. Too much clove in a recipe will overpower all other tastes.

**Ginger**—(Hindi: *adarak*) ginger may be purchased as a powder or in slices that have been dried and candied.

**Nutmeg**—(Hindi: *jaifal*) nutmeg may be grated into a powder at home, or purchased already ground.

**Baking Powder**—a rising agent available in most grocery stores.

**Baking Soda**—also known as sodium bicarbonate or in Hindi, *meetha soda*, this is also a rising agent, but it is not interchangeable with baking powder. Baking soda will bubble up when combined with liquids, and when it is used, the baked item must be mixed and baked right away.

**Buttermilk**—a soured milk product available in some grocery stores. An acceptable substitute for buttermilk is a mixture of half milk and half yogurt or curd.

**Candied Peel**—also referred to as glacéd fruit, candied fruit peel may be found in better grocery stores.

**Chocolate**—used for melting and making chocolate chips, bittersweet chocolate in slab form is available at better grocery stores. Any type of chocolate bar may also be used.

**Chocolate Chips**—sometimes referred to as choco bits, chocolate chips are small pieces of chocolate that are stirred into many recipes. They are available at better grocery stores and specialty shops, but may be made by chopping up a chocolate bar.

**Cocoa Powder**—available in most grocery stores, cocoa powder is a chocolate product used in many recipes. It is best to sift before using, as the small lumps will affect the final baked result.

**Coconut**—(Hindi: *Nariyal*) coconut may be purchased in a powdered form, perfect for baking. It is sometimes referred to as desiccated coconut.

**Corn Starch**—available pre-packaged in most grocery stores, corn starch is often called corn flour, and is not to be confused with the yellow flour ground from corn. Corn starch is a fine white powder used for thickening and binding sauces.

**Dates**—(Hindi: *khajoor*) you will find pitted dates in most fruit markets. They can be chopped into small pieces for use in baking and should be washed before using.

**Dripped or Hung Curd**—may be used in place of sour cream when partly dripped, or cream cheese when left longer. Curd or yogurt is placed in cheese cloth and suspended over a bowl. Refrigerate and allow all the liquid to drip out of the curd, leaving a creamy cheese.

**Flour**—There are many types of flour. White flour is called *maida*, whole wheat pastry flour is equivalent to *superfine atta* and whole wheat flour is *chakhi atta*. Flour ground from corn is *makhi atta* in Hindi, and corn flour in English.

**Golden Syrup**—a thick syrup made from sugar, available in better food stores. Honey may be used as a substitution for golden syrup if it is unavailable.

**Honey**—available in most grocery stores, honey is a natural liquid sweetener. It may solidify at cooler temperatures. To re-liquefy, place a glass jar of honey in a pot of cold water and slowly heat until the honey is once again liquid. When measuring honey for your recipes, oil the measuring cup first and the honey will pour out easily.

**Molasses**—a dark brown liquid sugar syrup with a distinctive malty flavour. Molasses is available in some specialty shops. If not available, a similar syrup may be made by melting *ghur*. (Full instructions are given in the Pantry section of the introduction.)

**Oats**—quick cooking oats are best suited for baking and are available in most grocery stores.

**Oil**—a light vegetable oil of any type will work in baking. Sesame, mustard and olive oil should not be used.

**Orange Marmalade**—a sweet fruit spread made from oranges and other citrus fruits, marmalade is available in most grocery stores.

**Orange Zest**—zest is the term used for the finely grated rind of citrus fruits. A fine grater will work, but you may also find a "zester" in better kitchen equipment stores. Be careful not to zest into the white pith, which is bitter. (Lemon zest is the same, just using lemons.)

**Peanut Butter**—a smooth spread made from roasted and ground peanuts (or ground nuts) peanut butter is available in most grocery stores. Natural varieties will have some oil floating on top, which should be well stirred into the jar. Available in "smooth" or "chunky," either will work in baking, but smooth is preferable.

**Poppy Seeds**—(Hindi: *khus-khus*) poppy seeds are widely available in shops where grains are sold. They should be cleaned before using.

**Pumpkin**—(Hindi: *kaddu*) this refers to the orange pumpkin, which should be steamed or baked and then mashed for use in baking.

**Raisins**—(Hindi: *kishmish* or *dak*) choose a sweet variety of raisin and wash well before using.

**Sesame Seeds**—(Hindi: *til*) sesame seeds come in white, light brown or dark colours and should be cleaned before using. The light brown are most suitable for baking, but white are also fine.

**Sugar**—for baking purposes, ground sugar or superfine (caster) sugar should be used. Light brown, dark brown, demarrara, icing sugar and other varieties of sugar are available in better grocery stores.

**Vanilla**—a long black bean, vanilla can be purchased as a liquid extract (try to buy a non-synthetic product if available) or can be purchased in its natural form. The bean may be slit and the sticky centre scraped out for use in baking. Many of the recipes in this book require liquid vanilla extract.

**Walnuts**—(Hindi: *akrot*) a nut sold in the shell or already shelled. Used frequently in baking, make sure you purchase fresh walnuts and store them in the fridge.

# *Index*